# Joy for Healthy, Happy Living
## Self Help for Happiness
## Gautam Sharma

gautamsharma.contact@gmail.com)

(This book is dedicated to my valued readers)

# TABLE OF CONTENTS

# INTRODUCTION

Have  you overheard people say" how can I find joy in my life, since life is so boring and tiring with the nine to five job and then doing errands over the weekend?. Are yourself looking to find joy but do not know how to or **where** it is? Sounds familiar?Stuck in a grind or in a rat race, somehow hoping for joy in the future?Many people know what they want to run away from, but most are not clear about joy and where to find it. What is joy ?Where is it?

Over centuries, civilization has defined joy in different terms and many famous saints, thinkers, scholars and subject related experts have disagreed with each other on its definition. Joy is defined in many terms:as rejoicing, contentment,euphoria, happiness well-being, satisfaction,serenity, being taken care of, ecstasy or the state of being looked after. This book describes joy as a blend of these in different proportions , different blends for each person based on personal background and circumstances.
However,among experts,there is consensus on some of its salient features. Joy is our innate divine birthright, it is the core of our existence and being the source, joy can be found,uncovered within ourselves and enhanced by individual efforts. Joy, like love, is a divine quality which expands when shared. Keep sharing it and it keeps growing and overflows from an endless source. Joy and happiness are both similar mental and emotional feelings but dissimilar in a way also( as are cause and effect)

since joy is the cause, always present in our core while happiness is the effect of positive and favorable events and situations. Joy already exists within the center of the self, within the heart and the brain and can be discovered, awakened and sustained since it is everlasting as Spirit. All of us can reach within and discover joy and have it shine forth with brilliance to light up our mind, body and spirit-possibly light up many others as well. This book may and will help you to discover joy and to share it with others for healthy, happy living. Let's awaken and expand this empowering,divine quality. Begin this discovery with enthusiasm to override speed bumps on the way- one of which is apathy (a common human trait which slows us down since it takes things for granted when things are working out well for us and as long as our lives are smooth sailing. Due to ingrained apathy,many of us start taking for granted our very basic blessings: that we are alive, that we have an intact body and mind, we enjoy food, water, sunlight and shelter, we can touch, feel, smell the roses and do other exciting things as benefiting from positive feelings and interacting with others and enjoying many other tangibles (family, money, house, car, job, valuables) and intangibles (love, friendships, status, personal skills, relationships, respect and fame) that we posses. Unknowingly we take many things for granted and fail to recognize, accept and show gratitude for important things in our daily living,which make up who we are and for all things we have and enjoy. Instead of being grateful and thankful, we get unnecessarily diverted and upset by small things, like some rude remarks from a stranger or even less important as not getting a preferred parking spot someday. Studies have proven that people, in general, recall unpleasant and negative events far more than the positive ones although positive events come about four times more than the mediocre and unwanted. Its surprising, that we often miss out on feeling and expanding on joy to feel healthy and happy, instead we get into unwanted diversions like negative conversations, talking about failures or about far away accidents or imagining doubts and fears. We have many positive experiences every day( many times more than the mediocre and the bad) yet we don't build upon the positives to enjoy and expand on them. A quick take away from this for everyone is to focus on thinking about as many joyful reasons we have today (our body,  mind, spirit,water,food,clothing, shelter , relationships and meaningful activities that sustain happy, harmonious living. For such precious blessings. The first step is to recognize,emphasize the goodness and be thankful for who we are and the abundance that we are experiencing now.  Being grateful, thinking positively and sharing love and peace with others are the building blocks for discovering and increasing our joy. It's also important to keep reminding ourselves that we are special, that we are here on earth for a unique purpose and we are rightfully deserving, worthy and valuable. Both wisdom over the ages and scientific studies show that a positive frame of mind, sharing love and being grateful helps to maintain high self-worth and self-confidence which in turn produces well- being and contentment.

Wisdom over the ages:

1." May you be filled with Joy and Peace, as you trust in the power of the Holy Spirit"

( from the Scriptures)

2." Where there is joy, there is creation, where there is no joy, there is no **creation"(translated** from the Vedas)

From as early as the Scriptures and the Vedas till recent research studies, joy has been recognized as a divine quality within us and has been well researched. Over centuries, civilization has defined joy in different terms and many famous saints, thinkers, scholars and researchers have differed with each other on its definition. Joy is defined in various ways: rejoicing, celebration,contentment, well-being, satisfaction, serenity, being taken care of or the state of being looked after. This book describes joy as a blend of all these in different proportions for each person depending on personal background and circumstances. However,there is consensus on some of its salient features. Joy is a divine quality, our innate birthright, it is the core of our existence and it being the source, joy can be generated within us for benefiting ourselves and others. Joy can be uncovered and enhanced by personal effort. Joy and happiness are similar mental and emotional   feelings; though, joy is the cause and happiness is the effect of positive and favorable events and situations. Joy already exists within the center of the self and can be discovered, awakened and enhanced; it can be as everlasting as Spirit. All of us can reach within and discover joy and let it shine forth with brilliance to light up our mind, body and soul-possibly light up many others as well for a lifetime of healthy, happy living Let's awaken and sustain our innate joy This discovery needs our enthusiasm to override speed bumps, in the way- one of which is apathy (a common human trait which dampens our  enthusiasm for happiness and positive thinking by making us take things for granted when life is smooth and all is working out well for us.  Many of us start taking for granted our very basic blessings: that we are alive, that we have an intact body and mind, we enjoy food, water, sunlight and shelter, we can touch, feel, smell the roses and do other exciting things for enjoying life fully and interacting with others and having lots of other tangibles (family, money, house, car, job, valuables) and intangibles (love, friendships, status, personal skills, relationships, respect, fame) in our lives. When we start taking things for granted, many of us fail to recognize, accept and show gratitude for important things in our daily lives;things which make up who we are and for all things we own and enjoy. Instead of being grateful and thankful, we  unnecessarily get  diverted and upset by small things, like some rude remarks from a stranger or even less important as not getting a preferred parking spot someday. Studies have proven that people, in general, recollect negative and bad happenings far more than the positives, even though  the positives happen  many times more than the mediocre and the  unwanted. Why do we often miss out on experiencing and enhancing joy,which should be  our basic birthright and instead get into other negative diversions like talking about failures, misunderstandings, celebrity gossip or about far away accidents and mishaps? We have many positive  events happening every day( four times more than the mediocre and the bad) yet we don't build upon the positives, enjoy and expand on them. The reminder from this analysis is for us to focus on thinking about as many joyful reasons we have today for a wonderful life (our body,  mind, memory, food,water shelter , relationships that sustain us and the experiences/pleasures we enjoy. For all our  precious blessings, the first step therefore, is to emphasize the goodness and be thankful for all that exists,  for who we are and the abundance that we experience.  Being thankful and grateful to the Universe and positive thinking are the building blocks for discovering and increasing our joy. It's also important is to remind ourselves that we are special, that we were born  for a unique purpose and that we are rightfully deserving, worthy and valuable. Wisdom over the ages as well as research studies have proven  that a positive attitude and feelings of gratitude to Divinity maintain high self-worth and self-confidence which in turn produce well- being and contentment. Furthermore, there is scientific evidence to  show that discussing successful and favorable events with relatives and close friends can quickly enhance joyousness and set off chemical reactions within the body resulting in increased physical and mental well-being and invariably,  healthy, happy living. The above mentioned findings and proven scientific experiments are logically understood by many of us, yet we are often hesitant to share our happy experiences and events with others, even with relatives and good friends,partly because superstition dictates that things could go wrong if we were to boast about good things (hence we hold back for  risk of loss of things should we start sharing our happy feelings with others.)By not sharing, we curb our happy state of mind, dampening joy(our innate divine quality) something we would ideally like to awaken and to increase. We may even be misguided into pangs of guilt for being vibrantly healthy and continually happy when many people are known to be suffering or are less fortunate and perhaps are not as confident as we are. It's quite a paradox that  although knowing a logical way to discover joy, we control and stop ourselves; we may feel guilty about good things  happening to us and turn to discussing shortages,   accidents,negative ideas or sufferings elsewhere. This book suggests that you should guard against the above superstitious beliefs and avoid being caught up with exchanging bitterness and complaints, talking about others' accidents and misfortunes Make up your mind not  to be influenced by irrelevant,  negative, discouraging media reporting. In short,describing your happy experiences to significant others ,relatives and close friends  is one of  the ways to let in the goodness of joy to  make you feel vibrantly healthy and happy. Human health studies' seminars on gratitude and empowerment highlight that making lists of the things people feel grateful about helps draw our attention to the positive happenings in our live s and improves our psychological and physical health and well-being. By using the simple method of writing thank-you lists and starting to express gratitude improves our ability to connect with others, boosts our willingness to help others, makes our outlook optimistic and happy, reduces anxiety and stress  and goes as far as improving the health for people with physical ailments ( even moderate to severe medical disorders) Studies on gratitude show that by verbally expressing gratitude we feel closer to people,  experience more energy and that helps increase and sustain our well-being. Keep it simple and easy:Several times a day,start with

repeating aloud uplifting phrases of gratitude phrases and write them down- feel the thankfulness growing within, until it becomes second nature and a regular habit for you.
 Joy increases when we share it with others. Given a choice,which would you prefer: to feel joyous, downcast or worse still  doom and gloom?You have choices and outcomes within your reach. To achieve a paradigm shift for joyful living, keep your mind coming back to pleasant thoughts,positive events, goodness in people things, happy news, the beauty of nature, warmth of relationships and intimacy,,hope for improvement and pleasurable expectations; hold vivid images of uplifting emotions in your mind and start acting as if you are joyous (whatever be your status or circumstances ) Joy is something that can be cultivated and sustained . Try these out and feel the difference mentally and emotionally: consciously choose joy, nurture happy feelings and continue to nurture joy every day. Experts have discovered that people who enthusiastically  talk to people daily about the good things that are happening to them start feeling happier and more content with life. It is an observed and a proven fact that, the greater the joyfulness  people shared with others on certain days, the happier and more satisfied they were on those days, largely because of the law of cause and effect : the action of passing on positive energy in the form of joyfulness resulted in feeling  uplifted mentally and emotionally.  uplifting. If you experience good things but do not share them it amounts to not having experienced joyfulness. So instead of just keeping happy news to yourself  in your mind,make it a  habit and a regular pattern of sharing joyfulness with those you are close to and comfortable with. There have been instances of remarkable improvements and solutions within weeks of starting private, gratitude diaries and sharing portions of good experiences. If you were to start listing and counting the blessings in your life, the list may run into dozens, perhaps

hundreds. To begin with there are many blessings that may be taken for granted , such us being alive with an intact body and mind, breathing fresh air,having water and food to sustain us,clothing and shelter   to protect us from the elements, having benefits which daylight brings, human companionship, relationships and a host of other tangible items and intangibles which make our living more comfortable. Showing gratitude for the present brings in more and more abundance and makes you complete in many other ways. Soon you will be able to recollect all that you have had Repeating this list every day to yourself will set up a positive mental and emotional energy field and you will start feeling more assured, more fortunate loved, lovable and worthy to the extent that most minor aches and pains will fade away, you will start feeling more energetic and empowered to be able to enjoy personal and professional activities with growing joy in your heart. This is a simple yet meaningful method of recognizing your oneness with Spirit. As we have come to understand it, joy increases when we share it with people who are close to us as first because it is one of those positive qualities which expands when shared, since the outflow of joy helps to pull out even more joy from our core within , which seemingly has an endless supply that keeps on bubbling up to the surface as more and more of it is tapped. Secondly sharing joy with companions, really close relatives and friends sets up a reciprocal cycle effect by which our companions relate to our joyful expressions and ,in turn, share their own similar overflowing expressions, overall creating an abundance of happy, healthy, meaningful emotions which keep increasing exponentially. An important part in this ongoing practice is to choose people who are like-minded , positive , helpful and will appreciate the exchange of joy, love, ongoing physical , mental, emotional growth with you. When sharing a positive experience, it is important to select helpful people who are open to helping each other out.

To sum up: Joy is that divine quality within us which increases as and when we can exchange it with others. Be proactive in your existing social circle for expressing your purpose or introduce yourself in newer circles and forums. Writing an article online or starting a blog may help you connect with people with similar interests and opinions. abundance of blessings and happy happenings with as many like-minded people who may be helpful and in turn open yourself to listening to and appreciating their expressions of joy. a This study may also help partly explain how people can stay happy and healthy through ways of keeping them encouraged for them to share their most positive happenings with relative sand close friends, and the things they feel grateful for. Supporting a relative or friend's well-being in turn may impact not only ourselves but the well-being of all the people connected. Most of us have a larger proportion of good news and positive happenings( on an average of four times to a single bad one) accounting for all good ones vs. an isolated mediocre event or bad news every day, yet we do not appreciate and acknowledge so much goodness in our lives. think of all good things about how we started the day rested and refreshed in our safe, comfortable home ,had nutritious breakfast , have an intact body and mind and work cut out for us and usually have in place ongoing relationships with others. We have so many blessings to count on: our body, mind, food, water, sunlight, shelter and many more of our tangible and intangible possessions. Still many at most times fail to appreciate many sources of joy. . In addition, we get very upset by some rude remarks from a stranger or we gossip about someone ease's shortcomings Why do we not build up on the present reasons for joyfulness, instead of getting diverted by far away unrelated bad news or some unrelated accident? Studies point to one explanation for this- the habit that keep us from experiencing, extending, and expanding our joy: our mind's in-grained thought process to think of the worst possible and to give more attention to the negative; has shown that we tend to remember bad events and refers to the fact that while we receive increase of joyfulness from new positive happenings, but over time, we get used to these happenings and such positives no longer have an uplifting effect.

How can we stop focusing on unpleasant happenings and instead nurture only the good ones evidence shows that relating happy events gives rise o increased well-being, fulfilling life contentment and physical and mental strength.

Such studies may seem surprising because we are often reluctant to talk about our good fortune.

 We don't want to show off about fortunate events or we may feel guilty that good things are happening to us in the face of the suffering exists for hundreds elsewhere. As a result we get diverted towards discussing gossip, sensational celebrity news or even accidents and disasters in countries far away. We can summarize from the above and confirm that describing our happy happenings to significant others and close friends does a lot of good and helps to spread cheer.

Some studies have shown that making daily lists of things you feel grateful for—which helps draw our attention to the positive happenings in our lives—improves our psychological and physical health and well-being. For example, gratitude improves our ability to connect with others, boosts our compassionate attitude, make us optimistic and generous, decreases envy and restrictive thinking even rejuvenates health for people with physical disorders and gastro-intestinal diseases in two patients)"There is research on gratitude to show that by verbally expressing thankfulness to people we are close to help increase and sustain our well-being (above and beyond simply feeling or writing down gratitude.) Famous saints, thinkers and experts have discovered that joyfulness increases as and when shared. Joy and happiness are two of our innate qualities which keep increasing as and when they are outwardly expressed and shared.

 Empirical evidence has established that people who regularly discuss the good things in life, as and when they happen, are normally happy and content with their lives. Share with those who care is a bold and joyous way of living which binds people together and can ultimately spread out as prescription for an entire community. Experts also found that, the more these people shared their joyfulness with someone on a given day, the happier and more satisfied they were on that day. It  was decided that sharing joyfulness caused this boost in well-being, either with a family member or a friend Those that share positive happenings and joyousness with other compatible people experience immediate, increased satisfaction and well-being, as compared to others who were not outwardly expressive and kept their news to themselves. Well shared positive happenings give ourselves a boost and set up a trustworthy mindset where others can reciprocate their joyfulness as well.

# *CHAPTER ONE*

Become aware of your dominant thoughts with the purpose of guiding them towards positive thinking. Your dominant thoughts embed themselves in your subconscious to create your beliefs and habits which translate into your actions and therefore create your reality. Review your thoughts, from time to time, to keep the happy and inspirational Regardless of the present circumstances, replace negative thoughts gently, lovingly with rousing, joyous, laughing, rejoicing thoughts-thoughts of love, peace, hope, compassion, winning and celebrations.

2.Write down, in order of importance, all your major strengths and your significant achievements till date. If you need prompting, ask a relative or a close friend to help with inputs for recalling traits and events and make this list complete with everything significant. Every day, preferably early morning or late in the evening,rewrite this list and read it to yourself because repeating these in thought and spoken word will make a deep imprint of your positive aspects on your subconscious.

3.Think positively about yourself. Remind yourself that, regardless of your low, moderate or high status in life you are still a special, worthy and valued person, and that you deserve to feel good and content about yourself.  Remind yourself that the Universe loves you and you love the Universe and that you are beautiful and peaceful in body, mind and spirit, just the way you are now. Your presence makes a valuable difference in the world, just because you exist. Instead of doing something greater than others,become a part of something greater than us. By attaching ourselves to an exemplary, beneficial cause, we are loved, loving and lovable. This book underlines deleting all negative thoughts about yourself from your consciousness, thoughts like : 'you are not good enough, not attractive enough or not wealthy enough. Replace negativity such as 'I make many mistakes" , or 'Not many people really like me with positive beliefs-and keep reinforcing:" I am important,lucky and fortunate, "I make a valuable difference in the world. To sum up:you are much more than just flesh, blood and bones,You are an amalgamation of mind,body,soul,thoughts,emotions, confidence, self-worth high goals, so ,build yourself up-to a higher level than just your human form( you being more than just flesh, blood and bones,you are a spiritual being within a human form with an energy field synchronized with the Universe); importantly you are first a spiritual presence with an intelligent mind and strong body. Think  in terms of being a magnificent expression of Divinity leading a human life.

4.Choose fresh, nutritious food as part of a healthy, balanced diet. Slow down while eating since meal times are special-even if you are eating on your work desk or alone. Switch off the computer/laptop/television, feel important by clearing the table and eat food slowly, with relish and gratitude.

5.Make it a regular habit to get enough sleep (aim for 7to8 hours every day). Instill joyous thoughts-thoughts of gratitude and thankfulness just before sleeping and upon waking up.

6.Clean and groom yourself regularly and well by taking showers, brushing your teeth and your hair, trimming your nails, keeping well-groomed and smelling fresh, wear clean clothes and use deodorants and fragrances as appropriate. Dressing up with style, finesse and finery will make you feel extra good about yourself. Within your wardrobe budgets and options , wear the nicest, cleanest, fashionable clothes- all this will keep your self-worth elevated.

7When you are done with work and social engagements, put on your walking shoes every day and go for a 10 to 15minutes walk either outdoors or in some indoor facility and work up a sweat doing cardio -workouts several times a week or as much as your doctor will allow.

8.Make it a habit of reducing your stress levels usingvery basic, practical methods. It may be easiest to follow self-taught options , learn relaxation exercises like deep breathing outdoors,or some form of meditation which is easy to practice for you, yet effective. Do all these as often as you can. You may also find relaxation with hobbies as tending to and watering your plants or playing with and grooming your pets or other exciting hobbies that makes you relaxed and peaceful.

9.Bring out items that remind you of your achievements and your happiest, memorable times, of people special to you and display them where you and others can view them often-these are to nurture joyous memories and happy thoughts.(constantly replaying happy thoughts and memories sustains joy and improves the sense of self-worth.

10.Add on to your routine some more things that you enjoy. Find time to indulge in at least one or two pleasurable things every weekend.

11.Take up creative activities: any enjoyable form of singing, dancing, art, literary pursuits will bring out hidden, normally unexpressed talents and help you communicate with your intrinsic goodness and help communicate with others lovingly. Take part in your circle of friends, local community groups, with courses, programs accessible to you for all related activities.

12.Take interest in your friends' and community activities to lend a hand and help others using your talents, energy, enthusiasm, your caring nature. Make some time for these late evenings or on weekends, because taking interest in others and helping them out will be appreciated and people will be grateful to you. Send out joyful, helpful vibes and they will come back multiplied. It's important to remember that what goes around, comes around. Giving and receiving is an ongoing circle of positive, beneficial energies- you will receive attention, gratitude and respect from others.

Always be friendly, extra kind and gentle to yourself by appreciating yourself, being happy with all decisions that you have taken. In fact, congratulate yourself for taking the best life's decisions in the light of your aptitude, training and circumstances. Celebrate important achievements and milestones and be proud of your value and worth.

Keep company of people who are important in life and mean a lot for you. In addition, reach out to network to meet more like-minded people and expand your contacts and connections. Social media communities are a possible start to get introductions and accept more friends into your circle .Facebook, twitter , linked in are excellent resources; use them productively.

13.Stay away from negative people who draw you down and with whom you cannot build up healthy relationships. You have started focusing on family, friends and more like minded people, so you can let go ties with people you are not comfortable with.

joyfulness and vitality (level of energy and vibrancy for

life).

joyfulness, love and appreciation. who did not When sharing a positive experience, it is important to select a helpful listener.

To sum up: sharing our joy increases joy. Telling people about our joyfulness has far greater benefits than just remembering it or writing it down for ourselves. The process of discovering, enhancing and spreading joy starts to help ourselves first and when expanded further can benefit other as far out as 3 degrees of our social connections(    benefiting our friend and that friend's friend and furthermore that friend's friend too and similarly keep compounding 3 degrees of connections for every close, appreciative and supportive friend , which will add unto thousands of people. In turn, others too can help support more people's joy by encouraging them to share their most positive happenings, and the things they feel grateful for. Supporting a friend or acquaintance's well-being in turn may enhance not only ourselves but other friends and acquaintances as well. A study suggests that we have multiple times more positive happenings than negative. Why do we not emphasize on the positive events and build upon the past to experience similar ones in the future?What stops from experiencing, extending, and expanding our joy?

Relevant research has been done and results may seem surprising because many people mostly hold back talking about their state of abundant lives. They feel others would get jealous because some get good things in life while a large majority get by with mediocrity and thousands-millions, around the world, even live poor lives. We do not  want to attract bad luck. Sometimes we don't want to be our own bad omen We may even feel guilty that good things are happening to us in the face of mediocrity and suffering in parts of the world. Dr Smith has shown that making daily lists of the things you feel grateful for—which helps draw our attention to the positive happenings in our lives—improves our psychological and physical health and well-being. For example, gratitude improves our ability to connect with others, boosts our compassionate nature, make us more optimistic and happy, reduces envy and greed and even improves health for people with physical ailments (even a major illness, for some people. It has been shown that by being grateful verbally we find others become loving and lovable, especially our family and friends and that we feel healthier and happier and it helps increase and sustain our well-being. Writing down and verbally expressing gratitude has faster and longer lasting benefits over just feeling grateful or, not feeling it at all.

above and beyond simply feeling or writing down gratitude.

The experts found that people who habitually tend to talk to people they are close with about the good things that are happening to them also tend to feel happier and more satisfied with life. They also found that, the more these people shared their joyfulness with someone on a given day, the happier and more satisfied they were on that day. To decide whether sharing joyfulness caused this boost in well-being,a test group was experimented upon and in objective terms it turned out that t Those who shared positive experiences with their companions and friends experienced a greater uplifting well-being than those who did not share their experience with their companions.

To sum up: sharing our joy increases joy. Telling people about our joyfulness has far greater benefits than just remembering it or writing it down for ourselves. This well-being influences that of those around us, up to 3 In turn, we can help support others' joy by encouraging them to share their most positive happenings, and the things they feel grateful for. Supporting a friend or acquaintance's well-being in turn may impact not only ourselves but the well-being of all the people connected we have three times more positive happenings than negative. What keeps us from fully capitalizing on all the good in our lives, making us experts have identified two main attitude that keep us from experiencing, extending, and expanding our joy: tendency to has shown that we tend to remember and focus more on refers to the fact that while we receive boosts of joyfulness from new positive happenings, over time, we get used to these happenings and they no longer have the same effect.

 Their studies show that discussing positive happenings leads to heightened well-being, increased overall life satisfaction and even more energy.

This studies may seem surprising because we are often reluctant to talk about our good fortune. We don't want to overdo " showing off" or we may feel guilty that good things are happening to us in the face of the others who are suffering in different parts of the world.

Sharing happy happenings with significant others and close friends spreads cheer all around and makes us feel more satisfied. with life.

Many studies have shown that making daily lists of the things you feel grateful for—which helps draw our attention to the positive happenings in our lives—improves our psychological and physical health and well-being. For example, gratitude improves our ability to connect with others, increases our compassionate feelings and make us upbeat and more positive ; cutting down on envy and greed and even improves health for people with physical ailments (severe disease in one case). on gratitude to show that verbally expressing the gratitude we feel to people close to us helps increase and sustain our well-being above and beyond simply feeling or writing down gratitude. known that joyfulness The experts found that people who habitually tend to talk to people they are close with about the good things that are happening to them also tend to feel happier and more satisfied with life. They also found that, the more these people shared their joyfulness with someone on a given day, the happier and more satisfied they were on that day. To decide whether sharing joyfulness caused this boost in well-being, the asked to write a positive experience or a neutral experience like a fact they had learned in class and either share it with their companion or not. Those that shared a positive experience with their companion experienced a greater boost in well-being than those who did not share topics of general nature) that enhance swell being.

. Sharing good news helps in a big way, though only people who are appreciative and at the very least good listeners. Staying away from nasty and negative people is a good idea in this context.

 Another relevant tip is to share uplifting, joyous news as early as possible and convenient because over time it would lose its exciting and vibrant impact. networking happier and more satisfied with life. They also found that, the more these people shared their joyfulness with someone on a given day, the happier and more satisfied they were on that day. This was the answer towhether sharing joyfulness caused this boost in well-being, experience or a neutral experienced a greater boost in well-being than those who did not share their experience with their companion or who shared a neutral experience with their companion. These findings suggest that it is the act of sharing joyfulness (and not of just thinking about joyfulness but not sharing it, or of sharing neutral information) that boosts well being. One reason that the study asked The study group The study group to share their experience with close friends or romantic companions may come from the fact that these people may be more likely to support us. In the study's last experiment, the experts noticed that received constructive, encouraging, enthusiastic and positive messages after a successful experience (high achievement on a test) showed greater signs of joyfulness, love and appreciation. A worthwhile point to keep in mind is that as more and more joy is generated, we have to keep it away from it turning sour, mainly by being appreciative of this noble quality and secondly by not exposing or sharing it with negative people who may dampen the good effects of joyousness. A worthwhile point to keep in mind is that as more and more joy is generated, we have to keep it away from it turning sour, mainly by being appreciative of this noble quality and secondly by not exposing or sharing it with negative people who may dampen the good effects of joyousness. When sharing a positive experience, it is important to select a helpful listener.

 them to share their most positive happenings, and the things they feel grateful for. Supporting a friend or acquaintance's well-being in turn may impact not only ourselves but the well-being of all the people connected The experts found that people who habitually tend to talk to people they are close with about the good things that are happening to them also tend to feel happier and more satisfied with life. They also found that, the more these people shared their joyfulness with someone on a given day, the happier and more satisfied they were on that day. a positive experience with their companion experienced a greater boost in well-being than those who did not share their experience with their companion or who shared a neutral experience with their companion. These findings suggest that it is the act of sharing joyfulness (and not of just thinking about

 When sharing a positive experience, it is important to select a helpful listener.

To sum up: by exchanging positive happenings, resulted in more joyfulness. Telling people about our joyous euphoria has far greater benefits than just remembering it or writing it down for ourselves. This study may also help clearly corroborate findings that have shown that our well-being influences others also,that of those around us, connected by three degrees of social networking . For going towards a long-term state of joyfulness, it's helping ourselves as well as others pursue not just for . In turn, we can help support others' joy by encouraging them to share their most positive happenings, and the things they feel grateful for. Supporting a friend or acquaintance's well-being in turn may impact not only ourselves but the well-being of all

the people connected to winner. No wonder , joy has been defined as a divine virtue because it expands and benefits ourselves as well as the entire circle of like-minded people as and when we share joy.
The abundance of joy, from an unending, limitless source, is truly amazing!

This studies may seem surprising because we are often reluctant to talk about our good fortune. We don't want to show off. Sometimes we don't want to attract bad luck to ourselves. Or we may feel guilty that good things are happening to us in the face of the suffering that exists in other people's lives. idle gossip and complaining, feeling negative or even gossip somehow feels more proper, practical and erroneously feasible. However, and colleague's studies suggests that describing our happy happenings to close friends and loved ones encourages and uplifts all concerned.
Many studies have shown that making daily lists of the things you feel grateful for—which helps draw our attention to the positive happenings in our lives—improves our psychological and physical health and well-being. For example, gratitude improves our ability to connect with others, boosts our compassionate nature make us optimistic and happier, decreases envy and

materialism and even improves health for people with physical ailments (lung diseases disorders, in two patients). new study, however, extends studies on gratitude to show that verbally expressing the gratitude we feel to people close to us helps increase and sustain our well-being above and beyond simply feeling or writing down gratitude. Wisdom over the ages has recorded with conviction that joyousness expands through sharing.

Experts have found that people who often choose to relate with people they are close with about the good things that are happening to them also tend to feel happier and more satisfied with life. They also found that, the more these people shared their joyfulness with someone on a given day, the happier and more satisfied they were on that day Its been determined that sharing joyfulness caused re-resurgence well-being,health and vitality experience with their companion or who shared a neutral experience with their companion. These findings suggest that it is the act of sharing joyfulness (and not of just thinking about joyfulness but not sharing it, or of sharing neutral information) that boosts well-being.

Those who shared their grateful happenings with their companion reported greater satisfaction with life, joyfulness and vitality (level of energy and stamina).
 When sharing a positive experience, it is important to select a helpful listener.
To sum up: sharing our joy increases joy. Telling people about our joyfulness has far greater benefits than just remembering it or writing it down for ourselves. This studies may also help partly explain studies by Rick Masters/ Ronald Simmons Being enthused with joy within , by increasing its flow to radiate outwards and around to other people, we can positively enhance the lives of people who are inter-linked up to three degrees of connections away from us, thus reaching a wide circle of extended family, relatives and friends within several social circles and unto communities at large and located nearby or in other cities as well. All those affected can in turn, can help support each others, setting up a reciprocal supporting others' energies resulting in a multitude of people strengthening their healthy, happy living. awareness of healthy, happy living. Supporting a friend or acquaintance's well-being in turn may impact not only ourselves but the well-Positive happenings occur every day, yet we don't always appreciate , recognize them and be grateful to

the Universe. Most of us have so much to be thankful about and proud of, starting with an intact mind and body, food, water, sunlight, shelter and people close to us-with many more tangibles and intangibles, yet a rude remark from a stranger or our missing a preferred parking spot makes us highlight the negative over so many positive blessings. ? A study by Tom Lewis and Pat Hartley suggest that we have multiple times more positive happenings than negative. What keeps us from openly realizing and appreciating on all the good in our lives, which is focusing on being happy instead of being stressed? experts have explained this oddity that keep us from experiencing, extending, and expanding our joy: the bitterness opinions and reconfirmation.; namely The bitterness opinions refers to our mind's innate tendency to give more weight to the negative; Adam Miller had found that we tend to remember and focus more on negative happenings. reconfirmation, discussed in studies on the evil merry go around, refers to the fact that while we receive boosts of joyfulness from new positive happenings, over time, we get used to these happenings and they no longer have the same effect. How can we counter this tendency to assign greater weight to the negative happenings in our life? A recent study by Sheila Cole and team-at a renowned university provides a clear explanation. Their study shows that discussing positive happenings leads to heightened well-being, increased overall life satisfaction and even more energy.

This studies may seem surprising because we are often reluctant to talk about our good fortune. We don't want to show off. Sometimes we don't want to attract bad luck to ourselves.. Or we possibly feel guilty that good things are happening to us in the face of the suffering in other people's lives; idle gossip and complaining, feeling negative or even wasting time and resources somehow feels like an appropriate, grounded escape, although erroneously . However,Ms. Cole and team's research suggests that describing our happy happenings to close friends and romantic companions is an important,helpful attitude for health and happiness.

## CHAPTER TWO

Many studies have shown that making daily lists of the things you feel grateful for(which helps draw our attention to the positive happenings in our lives)improves our psychological and physical health and well-being. For example, gratitude improves our ability to connect with others, boosts our compassionate attitude, make us optimistic and happier, decreases envy and greed and even improves health for people with physical ailments (intramuscular disorder, in one study). Ms Cole's new study, however, extends studies on gratitude to show that verbally expressing the gratitude we feel to people close to us helps increase and sustain our well-being above and beyond simply feeling or writing down gratitude. Psychologists and scientists have uncovered that joyfulness grows in sharing. Joyousness is one of the biggest divine virtues within us- we have to reach inside , awaken it and sustain it through our lives. B. B's. clarification "Let the joyful news spread out to all we know" Ms. Cole's studies provides empirical validation of their wisdom. Evidence also points to the fact that people who regularly tend to talk to people they are close with about the good things that are happening to them also tend to feel happier and more satisfied with life. They also found that, the more these people shared their joyfulness with someone on a given day, the happier and more satisfied they were on that day. To decide whether sharing joyfulness caused enhancement s in feeling good and wellness two test groups was put together with companions and close friends. On being asked about delightful experiences or mediocre experiences , they were responsive about their feelings during their testing sessions land how much they had benefited from them. their companion or not. Those who related positive experiences with their companions , directly experiencing in well-being compared to those who shared nothing or very little. did not share their experience with their companion or who shared a neutral experience with their companion. These findings suggest that it is the act of sharing joyfulness (and not of just thinking about joyfulness but not sharing it, or of sharing neutral information) that boosts wellness.

The study als    o had    severaseveral other sessions on long-term sharing the effects of regularly sharing joyfulness sustained over several weeks(three weeks as a benchmark).The testing contained writing regularly in a private diary about events they felt grateful for, or about neutral subjects covered during all test sessions They were then either given no further instructions or were instructed to share these with a companion twice a week. Those who shared their grateful happenings with a companion reported greater satisfaction with life, joyfulness and vitality (level of energy and for life). encouraging, enthusiastic and positive messages When sharing a positive experience, it is important to select a helpful listener.

To sum up: sharing our joy increases joy. Telling people about our joyfulness has far greater benefits than just remembering it or writing it down for ourselves. This study may also conclusively prove that our well-being influences many people around us,inter-connected through social networking unto 2degrees away We are ,therefore not just changing ourselves for the better but even influencing people unto three degrees of interconnections of social networking. Through a reciprocal interchange, others connected far away can influence our well-being and happiness as well. We can help support others' joy by encouraging them to share their most positive happenings, and the things they feel grateful for. Supporting a friend or acquaintance's well-being in turn may impact not only ourselves but the

well-being of all the people connected as a large group.
Joy is a true divine virtue which continues to expand
and benefit as we keep on sharing it with others
 We experience positive happenings every day, however
we fail to build a strong foundation to get ongoing
benefits. Analysis of this suggests that we have three
times more positive happenings than negative. However
we are not always focused enough to build on this
recurrence which should become our strength. This is
normally because of apathy and slowness to respond
when things are going well for us and life is smooth.
sailing. Also relevant is the human trait of playing up
the negative side of events, which when corrected can
become positive thinking and an asset for us. in keep us
from experiencing, extending, and refers
How can we counter this tendency to assign greater
weight to the negative happenings in our life? A recent
study by B. Brand colleagues at the Research Institute.
Their studies show that discussing positive happenings
leads to heightened well-being, increased overall life
satisfaction and spiritual enlistment.
Such fact based analysis may seem surprising because
we often hold back about talking about our good luck
and fortune. We don't want to show off, lest things go
wrong. Sometimes we don't want to attract bad luck. Or

we may feel guilty that good things are happening to us in the face of the hardships that exists in other people's lives. feeling negative or digressing to gossip and complain with other negative people ironically feels more proper, practical and comfortable. However, researcher Sheila Coleand team's finding suggest that describing our joyful happenings to significant others and close friends and is the proven path to increasing health and happiness.

Many studies have shown that making daily lists of the things you feel grateful for—which helps draw our attention to the positive happenings in our lives—improves our psychological and physical and well-being. For example, gratitude improves our ability to connect with others, boosts our attitude, make us optimistic and happier, decreases envy and materialism and even improves health for people with physical ailments (digestive malfunction, in two patients).Ms. Cole's new study, however, extends studies on gratitude to show that verbally expressing the gratitude we feel to people close to us helps increase and sustain our well-being and satisfaction in life above and beyond simply feeling or writing down gratitude. Wisdom over the ages has declared joy to be that divine virtue which keeps increasing as it is shared,freely coming out from an abundant source and truly as endless as Spirit. Ms. Cole's study provides empirical validation of their wisdom.

The research found that people who regularly to relate to people they are close with about the good things that are happening to them also begin to feel joyous and more content with life. The other conclusion was that, the greater the freedom in sharing good news with someone on a given day, the more the happiness and wellness was experienced that day. and more satisfaction and wellness that was experienced To prove that sharing joyfulness caused this immediate increase in well-being, researchers then got together an objective test group of a variety of ages and varying personalities with like-minded companions for an objective assessment NT in a testing area with significant others-and close friends. were asked to write a positive experience or a neutral experience like a fact they had learned in class and either share it with their companion or not. Those that shared a positive experience with their companion experienced a greater boost in well-being than those who did not share their experience with their companion or who shared a neutral experience with their companion. These findings suggest that it is the act of sharing joyfulness (and not of just thinking about joyfulness but not sharing it, or of sharing neutral information) that boosts well-being.


Next, the experts investigated the effects of regularly sharing joyfulness over a longer period (4 weeks in this case). New were asked to write daily in a private diary about happenings they felt grateful for, or about neutral subjects they had learned in class. They were then either given no further instructions or were instructed to share these with a companion twice a week. Those who shared their grateful happenings with a companion reported greater satisfaction with life, joyfulness and vitality (level of energy and for life).

One reason that the study asked to share their experience with close friends or relatives may come from the fact that these people may be more likely to support us. In the study's last experiment, the experts noticed that they received constructive, encouraging, enthusiastic and positive messages after a successful experience (high achievement on a test) showed greater signs of joyfulness, love and appreciation.

A worthwhile point to keep in mind is that as more and more joy is generated, we have to keep it away from it turning sour, mainly by being appreciative of this noble quality and secondly by not exposing or sharing it with negative people who may dampen the good effects of joyousness.

 When sharing a positive experience, it is important to select a helpful listener.

To sum up: sharing our joy increases joy. Telling people about our joyfulness has far greater benefits than just remembering it or writing it down for ourselves. This studies may also help partly explain studies by Pat Balog and Ronald Simmons has shown that our well-being influences that of To try to be happy may seem like a selfish attempt but it is a worthwhile goal to pursue not just for oneself but for our community. In turn, we can help support others' joy by encouraging them to share their most positive happenings, and the things they feel grateful for. Supporting a friend or acquaintance's well-being in turn may impact not only ourselves but the well-being

It has been documented that positive events happen to us every day, yet we don't always take full advantage of them. There is empirical evidence that most of us have many more positive events in our lives ( three times of positive experiences compared to the moderate or negative ones) and that we are blessed with countless things( the very basics of an intact body, mind, water,food,shelter,clothing, people, relationships and many more tangibles and intangibles,all adding unto reasons for joyfulness, yet we get disappointed with some small insignificant thing-its odd but is explained by inherent negativity in our subconscious and that while positive events are happening, we take them for granted and font use them to enhance our joyfulness reserves that it the studies by and Sergio Romano suggests that we have three times more positive happenings than negative. What keeps us from fully capitalizing on all the good in our lives, making us a slave to the bad? experts have identified two main attitude that keep us from experiencing, extending, and expanding our joy: the bitterness opinions and reconfirmation. The bitterness opinions refers to our mind's innate tendency to give more weight to the negative; Tim has shown that we tend to remember and focus more on negative happenings. reconfirmation, discussed in studies on the evil merry go around, refers to the fact that while we receive boosts of joyfulness from new positive happenings, over time, we get used to these happenings and they no longer have the same effect.

Can we outweigh the habit of highlighting negative aspects of life with happy, positive, meaningful issues?

? A 2004study by Nat Adams and colleagues at Oxford College explained the reason. Their studies show that discussing positive happenings leads to heightened well-being, increased overall life satisfaction and even more energy.

This studies may seem surprising because we are often reluctant to talk about our good fortune. We don't want to show off. Sometimes we don't want to attract bad luck to ourselves. Or we may feel guilty that good things are happening to us in the face of the suffering (omit) in other people's lives. idle gossip and complaining, feeling negative or even gossip somehow feels more proper, practical and erroneously can be done. However, Sheila and colleague's studies suggests that describing our happy happenings to close friends and romantic companions is a better idea.

## CHAPTER THREE

Many studies have shown that making daily lists of the things you feel grateful for—which helps draw our attention to the positive happenings in our lives—improves our psychological and physical health and well-being. For example, gratitude improves our ability to connect with others, boosts our compassionate qualities, which are within us and now revealed. happier, decreases envy and materialism and even improves health for people with physical ailments Sheila's new study, however, extends studies on gratitude to show that verbally expressing the gratitude we feel to people close to us helps increase and sustain our well-being above and beyond simply feeling or writing down gratitude. known that joyfulness grows in sharing. Happiness is one of the loftiest virtues B. B's. clarification "Let the joyful news spread out to all we know B.B. writes it." Sheila's studies are well documented and widely followed.

The experts found that , since the dawn of civilization, intelligent people have been continually sharing happy tidings with fellow human beings .to them also tend to feel happier and more satisfied with life. They also found that, the more these people shared their joyfulness with someone on a given day, the happier and more satisfied they were on that day. To decide whether sharing joyfulness caused this boost in well-being, the experts then invited into a laboratory with a romantic companion or friend. were asked to write a positive experience or a neutral experience like a fact they had learned in class and either share it with their companion or not. Those that shared a positive experience with their companion experienced a greater boost in well-being than those who did not share their experience with their companion or who shared a neutral experience with their companion. These findings suggest that it is the act of sharing joyfulness (and not of just thinking about joyfulness but not sharing it, or of sharing neutral information) that boosts well-being.

regularly sharing joyfulness over a longer period 5weeks for this study).they felt thankful for and some who communicated their grateful happenings with their significant others felt better, healthier, stronger and more satisfied with daily living (in fact with twice the test scores over others who did not communicate).
 The people who supported and appreciated the test group were selected because their significant others and close friends were the core group who assimilated and

magnified their emotions. This was empirical evidence that the test groups' sphere of influence reflected back the joy and positive emotions that the test group was sharing with the correct context of like-minded , appreciative and loving audience. that received constructive, after a showed greater signs of joyfulness, love and appreciation. . When sharing a positive experience, it is important to select listeners who we can relate to in a friendly, appreciative and supportive way. To sum up: sharing our joy increases joy. Telling people about our joyfulness has far greater benefits than just remembering it or writing it down for ourselves. This studies may also help partly explain studies by Irving pompidou and Ronald Strauss. Discovering joy , spreading it and sharing it with others has a far-reaching ripple effect within our social network- it benefits our well-being and contentment to begin with and furthermore spreads outwards to help others up to three degrees of connections around on our chain of connections. influences that of goal to pursue not just for oneself but for our In turn, others , through a joy discovery and sharing process can benefit bigger social networks and communities can help support others' joy by encouraging them to share their most positive happenings, and the things they feel grateful for.

Supporting a friend or acquaintance's well-being in turn may impact not only ourselves but the well-being of all the people connected to that friend.

The Science Behind the Joy of Sharing Joy

How sharing your good news increases well-being

Positive happenings happen to us every day, yet we don't always take full advantage of them. Discovering joy , spreading it and sharing it with others has a far-reaching ripple effect within our social network- it benefits our well-being and contentment to begin with and furthermore spreads outwards to help others up to three degrees of connections around on our chain of connections. influences that of goal to pursue not just for oneself but for our In turn, others , through a joy discovery and sharing process can benefit bigger social networks and communities can help support sleep, day? studies by BB suggest that we have three times more positive happenings than negative. What keeps us from fully capitalizing on all the experts have identified two main attitude that keep us from experiencing, extending, and expanding our joy: the bitterness opinions and reconfirmation. The bitterness opinions refers to our mind's innate tendency to give more weight to the negative; has shown that we tend to remember and focus more on negative happenings. refers to the fact that while we receive boosts of joyfulness from new positive happenings, over time, we get used to these happenings and they no longer have the same effect. How can we counter this tendency to assign greater weight to the negative happenings in our life? Sheila Cole at a renowned College discovered correlation between the two. Her research showed that relating positive events invariably result sin enhanced wellness, increased overall life satisfaction and boosts in vitality. This study may seem surprising because we are often reluctant to talk about our good fortune. We don't want to show off. Sometimes we don't want to attract bad luck to ourselves. Or we may feel guilty that good things are happening to us in the face of the suffering (omit) in other people's lives. idle gossip and complaining, feeling negative or even gossip somehow feels more proper, practical and erroneously feasible. However, Sheilas' research team clarified that by elaborating our joyous happenings to significant others and close friends, we can magnify joyful feelings and positive emotions.

It was also proven that the technique of making daily lists of things that make us feel grateful, helps increase our innate joy and that when we focus on specific emotions , they multiply exponentially within us. Joy attracts more positive happenings in our lives and improves our psychological and physical health and well-being. To state it in specific terms, gratitude improves our ability to connect with others, boosts our compassionate attitude, make us optimistic and happier, decreases envy and greed and can ultimately improve the health for people with physical ailments (gastrointestinal disease in several test group patients). Sheila Knots groundbreaking research also explains that by verbally expressing and sharing gratitude with people close to us helps increase and sustain our well-being above and beyond through simply feeling or writing down gratitude. have long known that joyfulness grows in sharing. In

Studies have proved that those who share happy happenings with relatives and friends felt joyous and had feelings of contentment on days they were outgoing and sharing happy news with other 90percent people from a batch of 200 surveyed felt satisfied and positive for a week at a stretch after they had shared happy news with others. Found that people who habitually tend to talk to people they are close with about the good things that are happening to them also tend to feel happier and more satisfied with life. They also found that, the more these people shared their joyfulness with someone on a given day, the happier and more satisfied they were on that day. Well-being and satisfaction comes naturally after we share joyous news ( be it about ourselves, our family or friends or even good news about the community)

Studies have been conducted with hundreds of people together with their significant others. These findings suggest that it is the act of sharing joyfulness (and not of just thinking about joyfulness but not sharing it, or by communicating community highlights) that increases well-being.

"There has been empirical research on a size able batch of people communicating with others for quite a length of time +(a month to start with). about happenings they were thankful about about vs random topics they read about as case studies, such a batch of people shared with their significant others and an analysis was conducted. The small group who were conversing about their grateful happenings and events important in their lives were leading life with contentment, serenity and were feeling healthier and happier with life overall. and had better health and more vigor in all they did.

One reason that the experts asked the study group was to share their experience with significant others or close friends may come from the fact that such people are more likely to appreciate, love and support us. On one section of the study, the experts noticed that the test group that received appreciative, motivating, enthusiastic and supportive responses to successful experience ( showed greater signs of joyfulness, love and appreciation. This encourages us to share our happy thoughts, your wonderful news and your successful experiences with relatives and close friends, keeping away from others who were known to react negatively and instead stay involved openly, since you are on a focus of sharing and increasing joyousness and don't want it to be curtailed by naysayers and dampeners. . When sharing a positive experience, it is important to select a helpful listener.

To sum up: sharing our joy increases joy. Telling people about our joyfulness has far greater benefits than just remembering it or writing it down for ourselves. This study may also help partially explain analysis that by has shown that our self-generated joyful ebullience can reach as far out as three degrees of inter connected social networking. We can equate this to spreading positive thinking and emotions to several inter connected social groups or **communities** spread over a large area, even in other cities and communities and countries. In turn, we can help support others' joy by encouraging them to share their most positive happenings, and the things they feel grateful for. Supporting a friend or acquaintance's well-being in turn may impact not only ourselves but the well-being of all the people connected to that winner, was right when he said, Joys one of the great positive things that multiplies when you share it.

## CHAPTERFOUR

 Despite experiencing positive events everyday, why don't many of us appreciate such good experiences and use them to build reserves of joy so as to keep healthy, happy, loving and satisfied? Experts as Bob Finklehave recorded that most have five times more of positive events than moderate or negative ones. Why do we not strengthen our health and well-being and improve our lives instead of remembering bad experiences? Finkle had isolated the cause that isolates some of us from experiencing, extending, and expanding our joy: the bitterness opinions and reconfirmation. The bitterness opinions refers to our mind's inbuilt inclination to accentuate the negative; has shown that we tend to remember and focus more on negative happenings. reconfirmation, discussed in studies on the evil merry go around, refers to the fact that while we receive rushes of joyfulness from new positive happenings, over time, we get used to these happenings and they do not having ability to keep our mental and emotional feelings upbeat and energized.

How can we counter this tendency to assign greater weight to the negative happenings in our life? A recent study by Sheila Cole and team at Oxford College gives answers. Their study showed that discussing positive happenings leads to heightened well-being, increased overall life satisfaction and even vitality and longer life( some cases from Okinawa, Japan)

This evidence may seem surprising because we are often shy away from talking about our good luck We don't want to boast too much. Sometimes we don't want to get ourselves bad luck We might even have pangs of guilt over good things coming in our lives in spite of hardships that is there in some other people's lives. idle gossip and complaining, feeling negative or even wasting time somehow feels more proper, practical and erroneously feasible. However,Cole and team studied the logic that describing our happy happenings to significant others and relatives makes us happier than those who don't do such things.

Empirical evidence exists that making daily lists regularly of the things we are really thankful about which directs our attention to the positive happenings in our lives—improves our psychological and physical health and well-being. For example, gratitude improves our ability to connect with others, boosts our compassionate attitude, make us optimistic and happier, decreases envy and greed and even improves health for people with physical ailments (digestive disorder,s in two patients). Cole's additional evidence goes further to prove that verbally expressing thankfulness to people close to us helps increase and sustain our well-being , instead of simply writing down gratitude or feeling warm and glowing within ourselves. Wisdom over the ages encourages us to joyously share joy with appreciative, like-minded people. Cole has provided empirical validation to such centuries old philosophy. The above scientists confirmed that people who are regularly inclined to talk to people they are close with about life's good events experience ongoing contentment and lead fulfilled lives. Experts also found that increased sharing of good news on a given day resulted in higher contentment right away on that day on a given in . Those that shared a positive experience with their companion experienced a greater boost in well-being than those who did not share their experience with their companion or who shared a neutral experience with their companion. These findings suggest that it is the act of sharing joyfulness (and not of just thinking about joyfulness but not sharing it, or of sharing neutral information) that boosts well being.

Do you sometimes wish what you could make your life happenings consistently joyous and successful? Do you feel worthy and deserving enough to be a lovable person having and enjoying a healthy and a fulfilled lifestyle? Would you like to boost your self-worth and your true value to their ultimate levels? Several types of people read this book:  first those with healthy self-worth, some others with low self-worth and the third kind being those with over-inflated self-worth. Individuals with low and highly inflated self-worth are both unhappy and dissatisfied; they are just different sides of the same bad coin (insecure and unbalanced). Low self-worth often results in not bringing to fruition what people desire. On the other hand, extreme, over inflated self-worth shows results faster and  seemingly easily but largely with  restrictions , mostly attracting people/things which are meaningless and  misplaced and  which cannot be enjoyed (situations ass mansion  but not a home, or  being in a  marriage  but without  mutual love and respect,  or  an  apparently  high-profile job  that materializes  but turns into something  unnerving and disappointing and furthermore doesn't last long).Although self-worth and self-esteem are a bit interrelated, they both have different implications. Health and personality studies link self-esteem with confidence (people's abilities to accomplish things, their general motivation and energy resources). For specific tasks such people are accomplished, take smart decisions, are capable and hardworking-they have self-esteem in their work. they are also confident with their educational background, their sociability and ability to lead, therefore they have high self-esteem about how they work and communicate. Different from this, self-worth is the self-assessment of our comprehensive value (to what extent we deserve goodness in our lives, the quantity and kinds of things/accomplishments, that we deserve, that we have good qualities and we have achieved good things).However, achievements are reflected in different ways : one way is material things(a compatible companion, a large house, elegant diamond jewelry, fancy new car, or other upscale possessions) ;other achievements are in terms of intangibles (leadership, fame, authority, respect, status, friendship and love).In order to estimate your own esteem, without over or under rating yourselves, start with analyzing what you find worthwhile. Reflecting on what really matters to you, deciding about these to fit  into your lifestyle (what is important and worthwhile), such an analysis may take a long time. The complete process is complex and can stretch over years the process can also get bogged down with events that cause us discomfort s we don't want or don't cherish.  Once done correctly, we can come up with our priorities which can serve as our personal positioning system(PPS) for where we are and where we want to go. Given here is an evaluation format which you may find useful to measure your self-worth and how to improve it. This is given in  systemic stages to help you connect with your own self-worth. Many have found this useful and benefited from it.  Let's use this practical, stage-wise format to measure self-worth and create a stronger and healthier foundation:

# CHAPTER FIVE

(Stage One) Think about what you admire in other people. For instance, you may admire people who show confidence, make friends easily, who are outgoing, good at conversation, influence others with their lifestyle (sociable, well-placed extroverts). You admire many other qualities, but to keep the evaluation concise, let's keep it to just one set of qualities. Keep in mind that this is personality analysis, so qualities you admire will be totally unique for you, it's not  whether it's is good or bad to judge by moral standards Also, what we admire now will  evolve over time (these qualities will be different 10 years from now) and will need re-evaluation after a decade.

Stage Two) Review what you wrote in Stage One and ask yourself: are some of these qualities in you too?

Stage Three) Mentally reaffirm that the qualities you admire in others, yet you find missing in yourself are areas of personal growth that will help you to strengthen yourself-worth. Once you define some things you admire in other people, check again to see if, at least, you have similar strengths. All that you lack are noticeable areas of personal growth for your healthier, happier self-worth.

Stage Four) With some quiet thinking, check within yourself what actions you need to take to build up qualities you admire but don't possess (by using a positive outlook and without feeling inadequate, at any stage) and then start taking corrective steps daily towards your desired goals. Depending on how low the individual self-worth level was set at, it will need that much correcting to boost it. Self-worth qualities are building blocks which can be assembled with the foundation first and upwards to make a strong structure of strengths. It needn't be toiling work or a chore to finish. We can make self-worth improvement as an ongoing, fun-filled and enjoyable process while celebrating each milestone and subtle growth and development. Surveys show that developing new, valuable qualities within ourselves pays off large dividends by lifting our self-worth levels up to their ultimate levels and feeling wonderful about ourselves now and for good.

Stage Five). Realize that worthwhile goals may take time and consistent effort to reach and to perfect; the process is essentially redefining oneself and keep reforming and evolving. Following the above example, if you admire confident, outgoing people but you are presently shy and an introvert, then start taking daily steps to boldly face your doubts and hesitancy, clean up your negative patterns, join public speaking classes, take help by learning from your outgoing relatives/friends, even fail a few times in meeting new people but be persistent, get up, dust yourself off and keep on going. Once you have reset your consciousness onto a higher level of boldness and confidence and you visualize yourself as confident and bold already, you will get more insights into how to achieve improved personality and habits. You have now set goals on what you admire, you visualize yourself getting to be good at those traits, follow the solutions that come to you and stay the course. You will get there and feel joyous and wonderful with your newly found strong and healthy self-esteem

esteem. Stage Six) Clearly visualize your new personality and how you would be behaving with confidence and your strong belief in yourself. Knowing you're worthy and acting like you are valuable are different. Quite often, we understand the rationale for things  but are not able to internalize it. However, by consistently synchronizing thoughts with actions we can achieve set goals.

Stages even) Make these a habit in your daily life. Once you have focused on and followed up on the above-mentioned stages, you will feel and appreciate a boost in your self-esteem and self-confidence. Keep focused on the positive, because whatever you focus on expands So expand on the positives of who you are and all that you have.  Give thanks and be grateful for the fact that you are alive, be thankful that you have enough air to breathe and since you can breathe, you can smell the freshness of nature and the roses. Be thankful for the fact that the sun, air and water keep all humans, other live forms and vegetation alive. We all have so many things to be grateful about.  the list would run into dozens or even hundreds and thousands. With the habit giving thanks and being grateful, you are increasing the flow of goodness that you receive. A very simple yet effective affirmation to repeat in your mind is: "I deserve the best, expect the best and receive the best right now and at all times". Say the above and believe that soul is all right and doing all right regardless of what is going on. Have ongoing faith in the Universe and you will receive abundance of goodness. There is so much abundance of what Divinity has granted you and the more you dwell on abundance and the goodness, the more you will receive." Conceive, believe and achieve" is not a mere slogan, it is the foundation for manifesting positive energy vibrations in the form of  material things Divinity has shaped this law for  all living beings from the dawn of creation forever. Thought process is essential for creating our constantly evolving lives. Your thoughts completely give shape to our happenings and to material things in your lives.

these with their matching significant others or best friends Those who related their happiest events with their matched person were brimming with well-being , full satisfaction and overjoyed with passion for living healthy, happier lives. along with companions fully content with vitality, vigor and ebullience.

The precise planning of selecting significant others or best friends was to pair up whoever was most appreciative, supportive, helpful and to avoid negative, discouraging people to experimentally share their experience s with companions or lovers may come from the fact that these people may be more likely to support us. In the study's last experiment, the experts noticed that received constructive, encouraging, enthusiastic and positive messages after a successful experience ( showed greater signs of joyfulness, love and appreciation. Evidence shows conclusively that happiness sharing continues to be happy only with appreciative, supportive Sharing with critiquing negative people dampens the euphoria and tends to unsettling and counter productive. When sharing a positive experience, it is important to select appreciative, empathetic and helpful listeners. Only. To

set the ground for mutually beneficial exchange, start by being the appreciative, empathetic listener yourself. After responding with enthusiasm to the other person's delight, you get your chance to build up trust for exchanging positively charged thoughts and ideas.
To sum up: sharing our joy increases joy. Telling people about our joyfulness has far greater benefits than just remembering it or writing it down for ourselves. Such study may corroborate that joyful sharing can influence up to four degrees of interconnections within social networks. In turn, we can help support others' joy by encouraging them to share their most positive happenings, and the things they feel grateful for. - suggests that we have three times more positive happenings than negative. What keeps us from fully capitalizing on all the good in our lives, making us a slave to the bad? experts have identified two main attitude that keep us from experiencing, extending, and expanding our joy: the bitterness opinions and reconfirmation. The bitterness opinions refers to our mind's innate tendency to give more weight to the negative has shown that we tend to remember and focus more on negative refers to the fact that while we receive boosts of joyfulness from new positive happenings, over time, we get used to these happenings and they no

longer have the same effect.

How can we counter this tendency to assign greater weight to the negative happenings in our life? A recent study by Nathaniel Simmons and colleagues at Oxford College gives us a clue. Their studies shows that discussing positive happenings leads to heightened well-being, increased overall life satisfaction and even more energy.

This studies may seem surprising because we are often reluctant to talk about our good fortune. We don't want to show off. Sometimes we don't want to bring bad luck on ourselves. Or we may feel guilty that good things are happening to us in the face of the suffering that exists in other people's lives. idle gossip and complaining, feeling negative or even gossip somehow feels more proper, practical and erroneously feasible. However, Sheila and colleague's studies suggests that describing our happy happenings to close friends and romantic companions is a better idea.

Many studies have shown that making daily lists of the things you feel grateful for—which helps draw our attention to the positive happenings in our lives—improves our psychological and physical health and well-being. For example, gratitude improves our ability to connect with others, boosts our attitude, make us optimistic and happier, decreases envy and materialism and even improves health for people with physical ailments (bone injuries in two patients). new study, however, extends studies on gratitude to show that verbally expressing the gratitude we feel to people close to us helps increase and sustain our well-being above and beyond simply feeling or writing down gratitude. Great literary figures have long known that joyfulness grows in sharing. In unless we share it." Sheila's studies provides empirical validation of their wisdom.

The experts found that people who habitually tend to talk to people they are close with about the good things that are happening to them also tend to feel happier and more satisfied with life. They also found that, the more these people shared their joyfulness with someone on a given day, the happier and more satisfied they were on that day. To determine whether sharing joyfulness caused this boost in well-being, the experts then invited into a laboratory with a romantic companion or friend. were asked to write a positive experience or a neutral experience like a fact they had learned in class and either share it with their companion or not. Those that shared a positive experience with their companion experienced a greater boost in well-being than those who did not share their experience with their companion or who shared a neutral experience with their companion. These findings suggest that it is the act of sharing joyfulness (and not of just thinking about joyfulness but not sharing it, or of sharing neutral information) that boosts well-being.

Next, the experts investigated the effects of regularly sharing joyfulness over a longer period (4 weeks in this case). New were asked to write daily in a private diary about happenings they felt grateful for, or about neutral subjects they had learned in class. They were then either given no further instructions or were instructed to share these with a companion twice a week. Those who shared their grateful happenings with a companion reported greater satisfaction with life, joyfulness and vitality (level of energy and for life).

One reason that the study asked to share their experience with close friends or romantic companions may come from the fact that these people may be more likely to support us. In the study's last experiment, the experts noticed that received constructive, encouraging, enthusiastic and positive messages after a successful experience (high achievement on a test) showed greater signs of joyfulness, love and appreciation. A worthwhile point to keep in mind is that as more and more joy is generated, we have to keep it away from it turning sour, mainly by being appreciative of this noble quality and secondly by not exposing or sharing it with negative people who may dampen the good effects of joyousness When sharing a positive experience, it is important to select a helpful listener.

To sum up: sharing our joy increases joy. Telling people about our joyfulness has far greater benefits than just remembering it or writing it down for ourselves. This finding may also help ,to some extent, explain studies clarify that our well-being influences that of those around us, up many distant linked connections. We may think it as self-centered to show joyfulness , however it is a community wide important element, good for many more than one person only not just for oneself To reciprocate, we can help support others' joy by encouraging them to share their most positive happenings, and the things they feel grateful for. Supporting a friend or acquaintance's well-being in turn may impact not only ourselves but the well-being was right when he said, "joyfulness is the only thing that multiplies when you share it

Joy

Positive happenings happen to us every day, however

we may fail to build up on these. We have three times more positive happenings than negative.

It is up to us to immediately follow up to strengthen our self-esteem and self-worth have experiencing, extending, and expanding our joy: the bitterness opinions relates to our mind's important capability to give more has shown that we tend to remember and focus more on refers to the fact that while we receive boosts of joyfulness from new positive happenings, over time, we get used to these happenings and they no longer have

How can we counter this tendency to assign greater weight to the negative happenings in our gives us a clue. Their studies shows that reporting important happenings leads to heightened well-being, increased overall life satisfaction and plenty of vitality

This studies may seem surprising because we are often reluctant to talk about our good fortune. don't want to display pride and perhaps, we may feel guilty that good things are happening to us in the face of the suffering that exists in other people's lives. Suggestions are that describing our happy happenings to significant others and close friends uplifts everybody all around.

Many studies have shown that making daily lists of the things you feel grateful for—which helps draw our attention to the positive happenings in our lives—improves our psychological and physical health and well-being. For example, gratitude improves our ability to connect with others, boosts our attitude, make us optimistic and happier, decreases envy and materialism and even improves health for people with physical ailments (bone injuries in two patients)Findings about gratitude to show that verbally expressing the gratitude we feel to people close to us helps increase and sustain our well-being above and beyond simply feeling or writing down gratitude.

The experts found that people who habitually tend to talk to people they are close with about the good things that are happening to them also tend to feel happier and more satisfied with life. They also found that, the more these people shared their joyfulness with someone on a given day, the happier and more satisfied they were on that day. To determine whether sharing joyfulness caused this boost in well-being, the experts then invited into a laboratory with a romantic companion or friend. were asked to write a positive experience or a neutral experience like a fact they had learned in class and either share it with their companion or not. Those that shared a positive experience with their companion experienced a greater boost in well-being than those

who did not share their experience with their companion or who shared a neutral experience with their companion. These findings suggest that it is the act of sharing joyfulness (and not of just thinking about joyfulness but not sharing it, or of sharing neutral information) that boosts well-
9being.


Next, the experts investigated the effects of regularly sharing joyfulness over a longer period (4 weeks in this case). New were asked to write daily in a private diary about happenings they felt grateful for, or about neutral subjects they had learned in class. They were then either given no further instructions or were to experiment by sharing good news with relatives or close friends week. Those who shared their grateful happenings with a companion reported greater satisfaction with life, joyfulness and vitality ( living life enthusiastically). One reason that the study asked to share their experience with close friends or romantic companion scan be correlated easily as people relate to people who appreciate them more .may come from the fact that these people may be more likely to support us. In the study's last experiment, the experts noticed that received constructive, encouraging, enthusiastic and positive messages after a successful experience showed greater signs of joyfulness, love and appreciation. A worthwhile point to keep in mind is that as more and more joy is generated, we have to keep it away from it turning sour, mainly by being appreciative of this noble quality and secondly by not exposing or sharing it with negative people who may dampen the good effects of joyousness. When sharing a positive experience, it is important to select a helpful listener.

To sum up: sharing our joy increases joy. Relating to people about our joyfulness has far greater benefits than just remembering it or writing it down for ourselves. This conclusion may also help partially explain the study by Irving Pompadour and Ronald Simmons which ha shown that our well-being influences that of those around us, up to 3 levels of separation. To try to be happy may seem like a selfish but it is a worthwhile goal to pursue not just for oneself but for our community. In turn, we can help support others' joy by encouraging them to share their most positive happenings, and the things they feel grateful for. Supporting a friend or acquaintance's well-being in turn may impact not only ourselves but the well-being of all the people connected to that friend. Joy, like Love comes from an endless source, the more we discover and share it, the more it overflows.

Positive happenings happen to us every day, yet we don't always take full advantage of them. Have you ever noticed that it could be a great day (you had 8 hours of sleep, it's the weekend, had a great conversation with a friend etch…) but that it takes just one harsh word from someone or one piece of that we have three times more positive happenings than negative. What keeps us from fully capitalizing on all the good in our lives, making us a slave to the bad? experts have identified two main attitude that keep us from experiencing, extending, and expanding our joy: the bitterness opinions and reconfirmation. The bitterness opinions refers to our mind's innate tendency to give more weight to the negative; Tim Wagner has shown that we tend to remember and focus more on negative happenings. reconfirmation, discussed in studies on the evil merry go around, refers to the fact that while we receive boosts of joyfulness from new positive happenings, over time, we get used to these happenings and they no longer have the same effect.

There is a way to overcome the negative and switch over to positive feelings. It is evident that discussing positive happenings leads to accentuated wellness, increased satisfaction for living and vitality and health .This analysis may seem surprising because we are often reluctant to talk about our good fortune. Our tendency is not to be extra proud. Or we may feel guilty that good things are happening to us in the face of the suffering that exists in other people's lives. idle gossip and complaining, feeling negative or even gossip somehow feels more proper, practical and erroneously feasible. studies suggests that describing our joyous happenings to significant others and good friends will spread good cheer to all involved.

Many studies have shown that making daily lists of the things you feel grateful for—which helps draw our attention to the positive happenings in our lives—improves our psychological and physical health and well-being. For example, gratitude improves our ability to connect with others, boosts our attitude, make us optimistic and happier, decreases envy and materialism and even improves health for people with physical ailments (digestive diseases in two patients)on gratitude to show that verbally expressing the gratitude we feel to people close to us helps increase and sustain our well-being above and beyond simply feeling or writing down gratitude.

The experts found that people who constantly are talking to people they are close with about the good things that are happening to them also tend to feel happier and more satisfied with life. They also found that, the more these people shared their joyfulness with someone on a given day, the happier and more satisfied they were on that day. To determine whether sharing joyfulness caused this boost in well-being, like a fact they had learn during life experiences and either share it with their companion or not. Those that shared a positive experience with their companion experienced a greater boost in well-being than those who did not share their experience with their companion or who shared a neutral experience with their companion. These findings suggest that it is the act of sharing joyfulness (and not of just thinking about joyfulness but not sharing it, or of sharing neutral information) that boosts well-being.

 Whenever we feel good about something in our lives and we reach out to share the good news with others, we come across some people who are enthusiastic about our success and this reconfirms to us that we have achieved something of importance and boosts our self-worth. There may be others who find faults with why and what we did and are clearly demotivating and downright negative. To keep our sense of self-esteem and self-worth elevated, it is best to screen out the people who react negatively to our success and achievements. When sharing a positive experience, it is important to select a helpful listener.

To sum up: sharing our joy increases joy. Relating to people about our joyfulness has far greater benefits than just remembering it or writing it down for ourselves. This studies may also help partially explain has shown that our well-being influences that of those around us, up to 2/3 inter connection network away. To help ourselves and three interconnected network away, we can inspire and motivate ourselves to be happy. To reciprocate, we can also help support others' joy by encouraging them to share their most positive happenings, and the things they feel grateful for. Supporting a friend or acquaintance's well-being in turn may impact not only ourselves but the well-being of all the network connected to such friends. Joy is one of the positive things that multiplies when you share it

## CHAPTER SIX

1Generally speaking,we experience goodness four times more than mediocre or negative events put together. However, we do not acknowledge and appreciate the goodness and miss out on opportunities to feel joyous from within This is inherent in our mind-set(dwelling for on bitterness and lost opportunities by keep on remembering the mistakes, the failures and mishaps while taking for granted all the wonderful events in our lives and all the good things we now possess) It is essential to get cognizant of this inherent human tendency and work on nurturing simple joyful actions and events and to soak in the love, friendships, relationships, kindness, compassion, pleasures as we keep feeling such joyful attributes. Every happy stepping stone , when appreciated leads us over a pathway of contentment in life, physical and mental well-being.

This studies may seem surprising because we are often reluctant to talk about our good fortune. We don't want to show off. Sometimes we don't want to bring a bad omen upon ourselves. Or we may feel guilty that good things are happening to us in the face of the suffering that exists in other people's lives. Quite the contrary as there is validation for describing our happy series of events to significant others and supportive friends makes all of us happy, healthy and satisfied.

Lots of research points to the that making daily lists of the things you feel grateful for—which helps draw our attention to the positive happenings in our lives—improves our psychological and physical health and well-being. For example, gratitude improves our ability to connect with others, boosts our attitude, make us optimistic and happier, decreases envy and greed, and even improves health for people with physical ailments (bone accidents in two patients). Ms. Cole's new study, however uncovers outcomes about gratitude to show that verbally expressing thankfulness has very all-encompassing and powerful effects which moves us and the people we associate with in exchanging thankfulness feel bonds of togetherness love and affection which in turn increases and sustains our well being- factors far greater than simply feeling or writing down experiences of gratitude. Wisdom over the ages has documented that joyousness expands, in exponential proportions when shared that In

Research along these lines found that people who photoelectrically people they are close with about the good things that are happening to them invariably tend to feel happier and more satisfied with life. They also found that, the more these people shared their joyfulness with someone on a given day, the happier and more satisfied they were on that day. To decide whether sharing joyfulness caused this boost in well-being. Research was conducted on a test group of about200 people -pairs of like-minded people matched with their companions-paired up as sets . The testing method was a set of objective multiple choice questions followed by a 5 minute private interviewing session with every matched pair The findings were unanimous-those who shared delightful events with their companions experienced many step wise increasing effect in well-being compared to all hose who did not share their experience with their companions or those who relate routine, unexciting experiences with their counterparts.

These findings suggest that it is the act of sharing joyfulness (and not of just thinking about joyfulness but not sharing it, or of sharing neutral information) that boosts well-being.

The study continued to diagnose the correlation with extended length of time(over one month, as the benchmark). The test group was encouraged to write daily in a private diary the experts investigated the effects of regularly sharing joyfulness over a longer period (4 weeks in this case). diary about happenings they felt grateful for, or about neutral subjects they had learned in class. They were then either given no further instructions or were instructed to share these with a companion twice a week. Those who shared their grateful happenings with a companion reported greater satisfaction with life, joyfulness and vitality (level of energy and for life).
One reason that the study asked to share their experience with close friends or romantic companions may come from the fact that these people may be more likely to support us. Sharing our euphoria over good news with like-minded and supportive people draws abundant joy from within us and such an overflow

keeps us healthy, happy and benefits others similarly also. When sharing positive experiences, it is important to select receptive listeners.

To sum up: sharing our joy increases joy. Telling people about our joyfulness has far greater benefits than just remembering it or writing it down for ourselves. The process of discovering, enhancing and spreading joy has far-reaching effects and implications- to begin with it benefits us with more vitality, better health and happiness and continues to benefit people up the link of family/friends unto three degrees of connections. By a reciprocal process, some companions and close friends , by initiating the spreading-the-joy process will benefit a combination of their own three degrees of connections. So, on an ongoing process through give and take interactions , several social circles will get rejuvenated, refreshed and buoyant with the joys for healthy, happy living. oneself but for our community. In turn, we can help support others' joy by encouraging them to share their most positive happenings, and the things they feel grateful for. Supporting a friend or acquaintance's well-being in turn may impact not only ourselves but the well-being of all the people connected to that friend. Many of us fail to realize that life has worked for us and so many good things/people have been in place for us, yet we do not appreciate them fully nor are thankful for them. To begin with , we are blessed with an intact body and mind, food, water, daylight, shelter Positive happenings happen to us every day, yet we don't always take full advantage of them. Discovering joy , spreading it and sharing it with others has a far-reaching ripple effect within our social network- it benefits our well-being and contentment to begin with and furthermore spreads outwards to help others unto to three degrees of connections around on our chain of connections. influences that of goal to pursue not just for oneself but for our In turn, others , through a joy discovery and sharing process can benefit bigger social networks and communities can help support sleep, studies by Suggestible we have three times more positive happenings than negative. What keeps us from fully capitalizing on all the good in our lives, making us a slave to the bad? experts have identified two main attitude that keep us from experiencing, extending, and expanding our joy: the bitterness our mind's innate tendency to give more weight to the negative; has shown that we tend to remember and focus more on negative happenings. , refers to the fact that while we receive boosts of joyfulness from new positive happenings, over time, we get used to these happenings and they no longer have the same effect.

How can we counter this tendency to assign greater weight to the negative happenings in our life? A recent study by RamonCruz and associates at a leading

Research Institute details the explanation. Their study shows that discussing positive happenings leads to heightened well-being, increased overall life satisfaction and even more energy.

This studies may seem surprising because we are often reluctant to talk about our good fortune. We don't want to show off. Sometimes we don't want to "jinx" ourselves. Or we may feel guilty that good things are happening to us in the face of the suffering that exists in other people's lives. idle gossip and complaining, feeling negative or even gossip somehow feels more proper, practical and erroneously feasible. However, Sheila and colleague's studies suggests that describing our happy happenings to close friends and romantic companions is a better idea.

Many studies have shown that making daily lists of the things you feel grateful for—which helps draw our attention to the positive happenings in our lives—improves our psychological and physical health and well-being. For example, gratitude improves our ability to connect with others, boosts our attitude, make us optimistic and happier, decreases envy and materialism and even improves health for people with physical ailments bone fractures for two patients)

. Sheila Cole's new study, however, extends studies on

gratitude to show that verbally expressing the gratitude we feel to people close to us helps increase and sustain our well-being above and beyond simply feeling or writing down gratitude. figures have long known that joyfulness grows in sharing. " studies provides empirical validation of their wisdom.

The experts found that people who habitually tend to talk to people they are close with about the good things that are happening to them also tend to feel happier and more satisfied with life. They also found that, the more these people shared their joyfulness with someone on a given day, the happier and more satisfied they were on that day. To determine whether sharing joyfulness caused this boost in well-being, the experts then invited into a laboratory with a romantic companion or friend. were asked to write a positive experience or a neutral experience like a fact they had learned in class and either share it with their companion or not. Those that shared a positive experience with their companion experienced a greater boost in well-being than those who did not share their experience with their companion or who shared a neutral experience with their companion. These findings suggest that it is the act of sharing joyfulness (and not of just thinking about joyfulness but not sharing it, or of sharing neutral information) that boosts well-being.

Next, the experts investigated the effects of regularly sharing joyfulness over a longer period (4 weeks in this case). New were asked to write daily in a private diary about happenings they felt grateful for, or about neutral subjects they had learned in class. They were then either given no further instructions or were instructed to share these with a companion twice a week. Those who shared their grateful happenings with a companion reported greater satisfaction with life, joyfulness and vitality (level of energy and for life).

One reason that the study asked to share their experience with close friends or romantic companions may come from the fact that these people may be more likely to support us. In the study's last experiment, the experts noticed that received constructive, encouraging, enthusiastic and positive messages after a successful experience (high achievement on a test) showed greater signs of joyfulness, love and appreciation.A worthwhile point to keep in mind is that as more and more joy is generated, we have to keep it away from it turning sour, mainly by being appreciative of this noble quality and secondly by not exposing or sharing it with negative people who may dampen the good effects of joyousness. When sharing a positive experience, it is important to select a helpful listener.

To sum up: sharing our joy increases joy. Telling people about our joyfulness has far greater benefits than just remembering it or writing it down for ourselves. To sum up: The ongoing process of discovering joy from within and increasing this divine quality benefits us plus it also benefits a whole set of people interlinked up to the third degree of connections outwards from us joy by encouraging them to share their most positive happenings, and the things they feel grateful for. Supporting a friend or acquaintance's well-being in turn may impact not only ourselves but the well-

Positive happenings happen to us every day, yet we don't always take full advantage of them. Discovering joy , spreading it and sharing it with others has a far-reaching ripple effect within our social network- it benefits our well-being and contentment to begin with and furthermore spreads outwards to help others unto-to three degrees of connections around on our chain of connections. influences that of goal to pursue not just for oneself but for our In turn, others , through a joy discovery and sharing process can benefit bigger social networks and communities can help support studies by

Shelley three times more positive happenings than negative. What keeps us from fully improving on all the good in our lives, making us a slave to the bad? experts have identified two main attitude that keep us from experiencing, extending, and expanding our joy: the bitterness opinions and reconfirmation. The bitterness opinions refers to our mind's innate tendency to give more weight to the negative; has shown that we tend to remember and focus more on negative aspects. Over a continued time frame of happy events, we get used to a flat, consistent pattern and stop feeling joy, although most things are rewarding, productive and happy. Continuous analysis and a shift to positive attitudes are the ways to keep joyousness consistently uplifting our body and mind.

 Sheila and Susan from Brunswick's studies show that discussing positive happenings leads to heightened well-being, increased overall life satisfaction and even more Clinical evidence can sound a bit odd, as normally Most times, most of us do not want to share our good fortune and good news that we are bubbling with inside and prefer to keep it personal and private to ourselves, for two reasons: not wanting to show off and thereby bring bad luck for ourselves and secondly not being sure as to how others would react to our good news. Would they be cold and distant? Or would they be suspicious or envious in some way? We are often reluctant to talk about our good fortune. We don't want to show off. Or we may feel guilty that good things are happening to us in the face of the suffering that exists in other people's lives. However, and that describing our happy happenings to significant others and family helps us uncover joyfulness and gives others a relevant opportunities to talk about their own wonderful events. Many studies have shown that making daily lists of the things you feel grateful for—which helps draw our attention to the positive happenings in your lives—improves our psychological and physical health and well-being. For example, gratitude improves our ability to connect with others, boosts our compassionate expressions make us optimistic and happier, decreases envy and materialism and even improves health for people with physical ailments (bone related accidents in two patients). however, extends studies on gratitude to show that verbally expressing the gratitude we feel to people close to us helps increase and sustain our well-being above and beyond simply feeling or writing down gratitude. Great literary figures have

The experts found that people who habitually tend to talk to people they are close with about the good things that are happening to them also tend to feel happier and more satisfied with life. They also found that, the more these people shared their joyfulness with someone on a given day, the happier and more satisfied they were on that day. To determine whether sharing joyfulness caused this boost in well-being, the experts then invited into a laboratory with a romantic companion or friend. were asked to write down a positive experience or a neutral experience like a fact they had learned in class and either share it with their companion or not. Those that shared a positive experience with their companion experienced a greater boost in well-being than those who did not share their experience with their companion or who shared a neutral experience with their companion. These findings suggest that it is the act of sharing joyfulness (and not of just thinking about joyfulness but not sharing it, or of sharing neutral information) that boosts well being.

 they felt grateful for, or about neutral subjects they had learned in class. They were then either given no further instructions or were instructed to share these with a companion twice a week. Those who shared their grateful happenings with a companion reported greater satisfaction with life, joyfulness and vitality (level of energy and for life).

One reason that the study asked to share their experience with close friends or these people may be more likely to support us. The process of discovering , enhancing and spreading joy has very beneficial, far-reaching effects. After getting benefited ourselves with health and happiness joy spreads out to reach other people linked to us unto three degrees of connections.( which is each of our close friend's friends) thus encompassing a wide social group. The beneficial effects are further compounded when other appreciative, like-minded people in our social circle also do the discovery, enhancement and spreading process which in turn radially spreads out to their three degrees of connections. It is however important to select people who are appreciative and supportive of each of our efforts because they become strong links in spreading joy to an entire community which can benefit from the efforts of several people.

To sum up: sharing our joy increases joy. Telling people about our joyfulness has far greater benefits than just remembering it or writing it down for ourselves. those around turn, we can help support others' joy by encouraging them to share their most positive happenings, and the things they feel grateful for. Supporting a friend or acquaintance's well-being in turn may impact not only ourselves but the well-being of all the people

## CHAPTER SEVEN
## 50 ways to discover and increase joy:

Life is a mixed bag. There are patches when everything works in our favor. Other times, it is a wonderful morning mixed with a challenge in the evening. Weeks and months of happy events at a stretch, then suddenly some mistakes or an accident, which makes us unbalanced a bit ; to stay calm and composed, regardless of what happens, remind yourself to react with peaceful responses to the assortment of good, mediocre and bad happenings.

 off track, but remember that most extenuating circumstances are temporary. Gain more clarity by staying the course and channeling your energy in a positive direction.

2. Trust yourself. Believe in your inner resources, no matter what, and you'll grow from the experience. I believe that the answers usually lie within and you are probably smart enough to figure out what you need to do. Give yourself a little time and have patience.

3. Once in a month or so, take ten to 15 minutes off in solitude to do some mental cleansing. Here are three tips to go over mentally during such quiet time: a) Forgive

and be forgiven by saying- I forgive myself for everything, in all spaces and time, I forgive everybody for everything and everybody forgives me. Now I am released and free and at peace. Second:I am willing to release all negative patterns within me, wrap them within love and let all negative patterns vanish forever"

4. Watch your thoughts. Your thinking will never be 100 percent positive. You must learn to dismiss the negative thoughts and stay open to other ideas that will help you move in a positive direction. Start recognizing negative thoughts and use your mind to quell them.

5. Believe that you are complete in every way: Learn to access and direct your energy towards the highest good for all concerned. Believe that your innate intelligence and capabilities can help you deal with anything. Self-confidence and high self-worth are important components for happy, fulfilled living.

6. Learn to love yourself. You do not have to be who you are today, and your life is not scripted. Changing how you feel about yourself means creating a strategy, gathering some new tools, and making yourself into the person you want to be. A good way to start is to stop doing things that hurt.

7.Temper your greed. To get to own many things can be

a propelling motivation for effort, however being greedy so keep levelheaded and aim for achieving good things without getting unbalanced Maintain moral and ethical norms for going after all that you desire.

8.Accept criticism in a cal and balanced way. It is smart to be dispassionate about critical comments.

 Recognize that disappointment is part of life. Even the most successful people must deal with disappointment, but they've learned how to use it to get to the next level of life. The trick is to process your feelings, then act

10. Deal with your hesitancy. Overcoming hesitancy makes you stronger, and being a little scared can make you better. You want to have butterflies; you just want them flying in formation. It helps to understand and admit your hesitancy. Then you can kick them to the curb.

Increase your Joy today-wherever and whoever you are. Start with these:

1.Deep breathing outdoors: Step outdoors, take in the wide, open vistas, appreciate the bounty of nature and do slow, deep breathing (As you breathe in, visualize taking in pure, white, radiant light of the Universe in and imagine it reinvigorating your entire body and mind. As you breathe out, imagine exhaling from within all toxins and bitterness out of your system .   Make this a habit whenever and wherever you have access to natural outdoor surroundings. Oxygen intake and the slow ,  deliberate pace of breathing will do away with your stress and bring your body and mind to an energetic, joyous state.

2.Keep that smile on: Practice smiling, as if you are pleased with yourself and all that is going on in your life. To become joyous, the biggest rule is : Act Joyous  The initial  make belief smile will start giving you enough reasons to be happy about. Whenever you can remember to switch them on, keep on repeating silently to yourself: I am the goodness of the Universe and I am grateful for it right now and at all times.

3. Ten minute walking: Being a lot  on the computers or electronic devices, most of us tend to skip the basic exercise that will be helpful for our well being. Remind yourself and follow up everyday  to walk for at least ten minutes at a stretch. Whenever and wherever you can fit 10 continuous minutes of walking, enjoy that time exclusively for enjoying the exhilarating feeling of your body moving in purposeful strides. This will give your whole body a good workout, get all your body cells in a

feel good condition and put you in a joyful state of mind.

4. Enjoy yourself and relish food and mealtimes: whether it is hurried breakfast time or a snack or a meeting over lunch or the dinner with a drink, maintain two common factors always -relish what you eat and be grateful for the food you are eating. These are relatively easy to do and work wonders for maintaining your physical and mental energy levels and regenerating joy when you affirm gratitude for good food.

5.Take a break from the routine, work from a new site, do your reading or work on the computer from a different place or outdoors,  maybe even from  a WI-phi wired café, getting away from the routine, reducing the routine boredom reason will bring in spurts of joy.

6..Listen to songs- Most of us can access songs sources and can use devices to listen to songs of our choice. If you don't have a specific choice or like several genres, switch between several types and experiment and enjoy what hits your fancy and gets you humming.

7 . Spend  time with positive people while working and/or during leisure hours. Positive thinking sends out

healthy and uplifting impulses to   trillions of your mind and body cells, shifting you to a joyful mood.

8. Positive Affirmations-perhaps the easiest, fastest and absolutely free joyful magical application. Start with simple steps and build this  into a continuous habit: keep repeating in your mind , in the present tense, that you are joy, joyfulness, goodness, well-being, health, prosperity

9. Play with or groom your pet

10.Maintain regular sleep times- go for 7 to 8 hours a sleep every night- a good night's sleep is the best way to recharge our mind and body cells and awaken fresh in the morning, re-affirm , to yourself, that you are happy, healthy, joyous and receiving abundance of good things in life.

11.No complaining:Stop yourself,every time you find yourself or you feel you may start like complaining- in many situations,either there is an option out , like if he room feels a bit cold or a bit hot, you can fix it by walking around or stepping out for a while to feel better. However, if its raining in sheets of water or snowing with multiple inches on the ground, grant it to severe weather and make the most of the indoors. A single complaint can perpetuate complaining, so without feeling sorry for yourself , find a way out of inconvenient situations and make the best of all circumstances. 12.Meditation-There are several techniques of meditation and meditation has countless benefits endless, but perhaps one of the more positive perks is what the practice can do for your mood. studies shows that allowing yourself a few moments of zen-like escape each day may make you joyful.

12. Law of attraction: Several approaches to this-visualize with as much clarity and detail your ideal, happy image and what you want your life to be; just keep doing this in an enjoyable, light-heated way because feeling tense and over-anxious doesn't work. Secondly, keep in mind that you will attract to yourself how you think about yourself, so think being creative and gifted, attractive, accomplished, working in fun circumstances and enjoying things and company of people which you would like to keep. You could change images in your mind as you go along and having defined the ideal set of circumstances, let go of them and let the Universe work out the details on the path you

have to follow to get what you want.

13.Help others, donate your time and money to those who need or ask for

What goes around, comes around. Our efforts to help others make others happy and gives us satisfaction and joyfulness. By the law of karma, help to others is rewarded by somebody helping us Not only will your kindness influence others, studies show it'll also make you happier, too.

14Spend time with happy , positive thinking people

Joy is really contagious. studies shows the more you surround yourself with positive people, the happier you'll feel.

15.Planning fun events , activities and outings:

16 Lightheartedness , laughter and rejoicing: Each of these are priceless traits to be cultivated using tools like sports, hobbies, plays, theater, music and social media networking.

17.Live in the present: Although planning ahead and scheduling our activities are essential for best utilizing our time to carry out personal and professional goals, font let doubts and apprehensions come in the way of living in the moment and enjoying every bit of fun and fulfillment.

18..Have fun exercising:

. Not only is it good for your body, but it's equally as beneficial to your brain. When you work up a sweat, you release endorphins, immediately raising your joyfulness levels. Go ahead, get moving.

19.Spend money on happenings.

A fulfilling life doesn't lie in our possessions, it's found in the happenings we have and the people we share them with. If you're going to spend some money, spend it on a trip, a concert or any other experience that will bring you joy. Science says you'll be happier in the long run.

20. Challenge yourself.

Work for that promotion or take on that marathon. It's a lovely treat for your mind, according to Gretchen Rubin, author of The joyfulness Project. "Challenge and novelty are key elements of joyfulness," Rubin wrote in Real Simple. "The brain is stimulated by surprise, and successfully dealing with an unexpected situation gives a powerful sense of satisfaction."

## 21. Smiling

Make believe that somebody is taking your photograph. Put on your best , smile as many times a day you as you get aware that smiling is beneficial. If the smile doesn;t come on easily, think of any joke you shared with friends- recalling moments which were lighthearted, playful, spontaneous may make you chuckle, the very least they will help you put on a smile for yourself. Psychologists confirm that just by faking smiles many times during the day, help stretch facial and neck muscles and relieve stress. With spontaneous smiling, we can elevate our moods, become lighthearted enough to share and appreciate the lighter side of life and keep our mood buoyant.

## 22.Enjoy the outdoors.

Take advantage of your backyard or stroll a park you've never been to before and thank yourself later. One study found that going for a brief walk in nature can help improve your mood and alleviate stress.

## 23.Make some new friends.

studies shows making friends increases our joyfulness and well-being. Join a club, talk to your coworker or strike up a conversation in the grocery line — you never know what kinds of new connections you can make.

24.. Drink a glass of milk.

Dairy contains Aristophanes, an essential amino acid that helps create serotonin, the "happy" chemical in the brain. Milk: It not only does the body good, it does the brain good too.

25..Keep in close touch with nature

Feel the simple joy of walking barefoot on clean, freshly mowed grass or get the tingling feeling of walking on clean sand during a stroll along the beach. Take in the fresh air and the calm as you listen to the sounds of nature. Enjoying the beauty of nature in most panoramas, landscapes and formations is the best prescription for relieving boredom, stress, cynicism. Access to nature is easy , free and in abundance, so go enjoy nature as much as you can. Take some friend or pet along too and experience the euphoria of freedom, joyousness, well-being and vitality surge into you.

26.Doze off for short power naps once in a while.

While safely on a train ride home or during lunch time on the park bench, doze off for ten minutes or so. You will be amazed with the refreshed rejuvenated self and the wonders of doing away with fatigue and stress as you wake up with a clear mind and energy surplus for the rest of the day.

 slows down our cognitive processes and increases the risk of depression. Try hitting the pillow 30 minutes earlier each night or taking a nap in the middle of the day.

27..Celebrate milestones-big or small.

28 Compliment others: One of the simplest forms of feeling good is to complement others and appreciate something about what they do:

29.Positive talk at the mirror

30.Meditation


Subscribe to The Good Life email.

No moon dust. No B.S. Just a completely essential daily guide to achieving the good life.

31.Give someone else a compliment.

Your generosity will make your day and theirs. Looking for a way to give praise that isn't superficial? Here are some ideas.

32. Find the perfect temperature.

The weather outside has a direct influence on how we feel on the inside. One study found that joyfulness is maximized at an approximate 57 degrees Fahrenheit.

33.Keep a one-sentence private diary.

Sometimes the most mundane moments turn out to be the loveliest source of joyfulness. studies shows recording these everyday events may make us happier later on because we appreciate them a lot more when they're revisited. In other words, if you ate a scrumptious chocolate brownie on Wednesday, write it down.

34.Stop to smell the flowers, literally.

 One study on how scent affects joy found that who were in a floral-scented room selected three times as many joyfulness-related terms than negative terms.

35.Lots of safe, pleasurable sex.

A good way to express your fun, passionate, playful, creative personality. Sexologists confirm that there is no minimum, average or maximum number of times or length of time-different people have different norms, routines and opportunities but good, clean, pleasurable,caring, sharing sexual encounters relax the body and mind, lift the spirits and help enhance health and happiness.

36.Plan interesting events: Weekends and holidays are perfect for doing fun things.plan to go discover some park, a hiking trail, pond or stream or the beach. Check out the weather forecast, the best way to reach your destination,what to wear and things to pack. Include some like -minded person ,if available. Looking forward to and later enjoying fun activities is inherently relaxing and produces body hormones that make us happy, lighthearted and rejuvenated.

37.. Release stress: you can begin anywhere and with any simple pastime- a dartboard, punching bag, skipping rope, tossing a smurf ball or a balloon. You may find advanced methods interesting as well- yoga,

Pilates, meditation. Have fun with whatever you experiment with or pick up long-term and surprise your family or friends with a friendlier, relaxed, happier you.

38.Praying

At times when life seems difficult and future outcomes seem uncertain, many of us turn to praying for things to work out well. Ever since the dawn of civilization, humans have turned their eyes and minds upwards to the Cosmos to grant them their wishes. Simply stated, prayers have worked for billions and they give confidence to the seeker that things will improve. Whatever our personal religious beliefs, there is evidence that prayers can improve our well being, health and joyfulness and help achieve many tangibles and intangibles.

39.Forgiveness: The act of forgiving oneself and forgiving others helps ourselves detach from remorse and grudges that have lingered on in our subconscious, although events have been long past over. Unless we get rid of the baggage that many of us carry around for long, we will be unable to work fully on improving our health and joyfulness. It is very important to forgive ourselves and others for everything with conscious spoken intentions. After forgiving everybody and everything , it is best to conclude the forgiving process by accepting that we are free and released and we are at peace.

40.Releasing bitterness: Most of us have read about, experienced and learn that adopting positive thinking acts as a catalyst towards achieving our goals, dreams and desires. The additional factor about this is to release bitterness , which many of us have unknowingly embedded in our subconscious. Time for some spring cleaning to eject negative patterns sunk in mostly subconscious levels. This is best done in solitude with very specific spoken and written intentions that you are releasing all negative patterns from deep within and letting them go far away into nothingness. You guessed it, you will after some sessions start feeling crystal clear and clean and that's when you can start with inviting positive thoughts and positive belief paternoster your conscious and subconscious mind.

41.. Art supplies

pick up some art supplies: art paper, crayons, paper

painting set and make time for 5/10 minutes for sketching/coloring whatever comes to you as natural inspiration-the sun, car, a human , dog , cat, clouds or a pond or boat , maybe a single flower. This simple activity will start your creative juices flowing and get you in a relaxed, happy state of mind.40 percent of us take to sketching and art as a hobby well into adulthood and most of them reported to studies that they had reduced minor ailments as migraines, heartburn and high blood pressure levels

42.Positive thinking reinforcement-.repeat positive affirmations to yourself, starting right from the time you wake up and during the day, whenever you are not busy talking or communicating with others or focused on time with family, eating, driving or working. You can either create your own positive affirmations or find some online (encouraging, uplifting thoughts even if some of them are exaggerated or seemingly out of reach). Search for phrases which will bring meaning to understudies show having a mantra can help with bad feelings. Find yours!

43.Love your self:Loving oneself is not getting on an ego trip, but it's mainly taking care of oneself, being gentle and kind and building up self-worth , which is an inherent evaluation about what we are worth and how much we deserve in our personal and professional lives. Be gentle , kind and loving to yourself, with no remorse or feelings of guilt and no regrets anytime. Whatever we have done and will do at all times and places was best at that moment of time with the information, aptitude and resources we have available under the circumstances. Moreover, we can only love others after we start and keep loving ourselves.

44 Love what you do and do what you love: many of us have evaluated several options and are doing what we love and what suits us most. If you are stuck in a dead-end job or career, seek options and opportunities to switch when the time comes, but loving what you are doing at the moment will give you satisfaction about your commitment and work value system.

45. Walking ten minutes everyday- loosen up your muscles and joints and feel the joy as your organs function optimally Walking releases endorphins into your blood stream and make you feel joyful and energetic. Its more than what the doctor ordered, it's a

refreshing way to have fun too.

The next time someone judges you for taking one of those infamous front-facing photos, show them this: A 2016 study found that selfies actually increase confidence and make you happier.

46.Meeting new, like-minded people: Get personal, beyond phone calls, texts and e-mails and meet new, like-minded people. Getting, giving and sharing new perspectives is refreshing-many times joyous and results in healthy living. Research studies shows we simply feel better when we're around lively, positive other people.

47.Power of prayers:Whatever your heritage, community or faith and whatever name you grant God:creator of the universe, the Supreme Being, God,Universe Divinity, Spirit, in moments of need or as a regular practice reach out and ask for what you seek and ask for help in the form of prayers..Millions have asked for and received help. Believe in the power of prayer and to those who pray regularly, nothing will be denied. Prayers are the surest ways for discovering and increasing joy and for healthy, happy living.

48.Positive Thinking, Power of Optimism

If you think you can, you will. If you think you cant, you wont. Go for the things that you want with a positive attitude and celebrate on receiving all things you focus on. lining in any situation. Optimists are not only more joyful, they also may live longer. That's a lot of extra time to be happy.

49. Hum for 30 seconds any of your favorite, happy songs You will instantly feel a joyous uplift. Try to make this a habit, by remembering few songs that make you feel good and hum these as and when you get a chance. Keep that momentum going for keeping lighthearted, happy and confident using as many waysasyou have learned.

50. Have faith in Divinity: this point underlines everything you do in life .You are alive, blessed Divinity has brought you intact so far in your life, so trust in Spirit to help you continue forward and sustain your joy and well-being.

# ABOUT THE AUTHOR

Positive Thinking Mentor Author Gautam Sharma (an intelligent, accomplished, capable,creative professional)has lived in Asia, Europe, Africa and now living in USA embodies and edifies positive thinking , power of optimism and is sharing insights into human behavior and human potential through philosophical, psychological perspectives with the view of sharing mankind's centuries-old wisdom plus proven, studies findings so as to empower people worldwide. The author plans to utilize his strengths of professionalism,wide,varied experience, creativity and communications' skills to publish the Empowerment Series on improvement, self-help topics. Thank you valued readers for your continuous support , contributions and your favorable feedback. Wishing everybody abundance of positive thinking and better living through the power of optimism.

## Other books written by the Author, Gautam Sharma

### Positive Thinking, Power of Optimism

https://www.amazon.com/POSITIVE-THINKING-OPTIMISM-Original-English-ebook/dp/B01HRY684S

and

## Self-Confidence, Self-Esteem for Healthy, Happy Living

https://www.amazon.com/Self-Confidence-Esteem-joyfulness-Success/dp/B07846PDMT/ref=tmm_aud_title_0?_encoding=UTF8&qid=&sr=

www.ingramcontent.com/pod-product-compliance
Lightning Source LLC
Chambersburg PA
CBHW070817260726
48660CB00005B/1884